Ohio Notary Public Exam

"You never fail until you stop trying" - Albert Einstein

For inquiries;
info@xmprep.com

Unauthorised copying of any part of this test is illegal.

Ohio Notary Public Exam #1

Test Taking Tips

☐ Take a deep breath and relax

☐ Read directions carefully

☐ Read the questions thoroughly

☐ Make sure you understand what is being asked

☐ Go over all of the choices before you answer

☐ Paraphrase the question

☐ Eliminate the options you know are wrong

☐ Check your work

☐ Think positively and do your best

Table of Contents

Section 1	
DIRECTION	1
PRACTICE TEST	2 - 12
ANSWER KEY	13
Section 2	
DIRECTION	14
PRACTICE TEST	15 - 25
ANSWER KEY	26
Section 3	
DIRECTION	27
PRACTICE TEST	28 - 42
ANSWER KEY	43

Copyright © Educational Testing Group, All rights reserved.
This booklet may not be reproduced and transmitted in any form by any means without the permission of the publisher.
This booklet has been prepared and printed in USA.

TEST DIRECTION

DIRECTIONS

Read the questions carefully and then choose the ONE best answer to each question.

Be sure to allocate your time carefully so you are able to complete the entire test within the testing session. You may go back and review your answers at any time.

You may use any available space in your test booklet for scratch work.

Questions in this booklet are not actual test questions but they are the samples for commonly asked questions.

This test aims to cover all topics which may appear on the actual test. However some topics may not be covered.

Studying this booklet will be preparing you for the actual test. It will not guarantee improving your test score but it will help you pass your exam on the first attempt.

Some useful tips for answering multiple choice questions;

- Start with the questions that you can easily answer.

- Underline the keywords in the question.

- Be sure to read all the choices given.

- Watch for keywords such as NOT, always, only, all, never, completely.

- Do not forget to answer every question.

1

If a person has been convicted of a felony, he may not be appointed as a notary public in which of the following?

A) Any state of the United States
B) The county of jurisdiction
C) Any place in the world
D) Some states of the United States

2

How much can a notary request for administering an oath to a military officer, public official, or public employee?

A) 75¢
B) $2.00
C) $4.00
D) Nothing

3

Which of the following appoints and commissions notaries in public?

A) Attorney General
B) Governor Authority
C) Secretary of State
D) Office of General Services

4

Which of the following describes the individuals who are commissioned as a notary public?

A) They must be native-born citizens
B) They must have high school diplomas
C) They are commissioned at the discretion of the Secretary of State
D) They must have some legal background

5

Which of the following happens if an appointee does not file his oath of office within the specified period?

A) The fee is refunded
B) The appointment is revoked
C) The appointee is guilty of a misdemeanor
D) The appointee can not apply for a new appointment for at least one month

6

Which of the following is a crime, typically one involving violence, punishable by imprisonment in a state prison?

A) Felony
B) Perjury Crime
C) Misdemeanor
D) Criminal Offense

CONTINUE ▶

7

The origination of a useless certificate and the collection of a fee therefore after receipt of notice that such practices must be discontinued justifies which of the following finding?

A) Misfeasance
B) Malpractice
C) Insubordination
D) Misconduct

8

A person who communicates by telephone or mail in a manner to cause annoyance or alarm is guilty of which of the following?

A) Felony
B) Assault
C) Battery
D) Harassment

9

A notary public is NOT allowed to administer an oath to which of the following?

A) Military officers
B) Public officials
C) Family members
D) Himself

10

Which of the following is the prime duty of a Notary Public?

A) To serve the public as an impartial witness when relevant documents are signed; administer oaths, and take proof and acknowledgment of written instruments.
B) To attest to the genuineness of any deeds or writings to render them available as evidence of the facts therein contained.
C) To take acknowledge of or proof of the execution of an instrument by the client.
D) To attest to the genuineness of notice, in that one who is entitled to notice of a fact, will thus be bound by acquiring knowledge of it.

11

A legislature is a deliberative assembly with authority to make laws for a political entity such as a country or city.

Which of the following is the name given to the laws which are passed by legislatures?

A) Bill
B) Statute
C) Contract
D) Code

12

Which of the following must a Notary do?

A) Keep a copy of every document notarized.
B) Keep the stamp and journal under his direct control.
C) Send the copy of the notarized document to the State.
D) All of the above

13

Which of the following documents does not require a seal?

A) The subdivision map
B) The certificate of veterans
C) The circulator's affidavit
D) The change of venue

14

Which of the following can non-resident notaries do?

A) Notarize wills and trusts
B) Execute certified copies
C) Administer protests of note
D) Take depositions

15

What is the name given to the part of a notary certificate that provides the location of where the notarial act was performed?

A) Scilicet
B) Venue
C) Testimonial clause
D) Verification

16

Certificates of acknowledgment or proof are not entitled to be read in evidence or recorded in this state if they are made in a foreign country other than which of the following?

A) United Kingdom
B) Canada
C) Guam
D) Mexico

17

A notary public can not give legal consultation except when he

A) makes known the fact that he is not an attorney
B) does not collect a fee
C) has a law degree
D) none of the above

18

A notary who is appointed under the name of Mary K. Jones may sign as which of the following?

A) Mary K. Jones
B) M. Jones
C) M.K. Jones
D) All of the above

19

Which of the following is the process of taking an argument between people or groups to a court of law?

A) Compromise
B) Litigation
C) Protestation
D) Perjury

20

Which of the following given below is not mandatory for the notary to use?

A) Signature
B) Jurat
C) Venue
D) Seal

21

When taking an oath what should the signer do?

A) Must raise right hand
B) Must pay an extra fee
C) Must repeat oath
D) It is not required to raise the right hand.

22

Which of the following can prevent an individual from becoming a notary public?

A) Holding another public office
B) Being a commissioned military officer
C) Being a retired public employee
D) Being a minor

23

It is a certificate issued by the Secretary of State that proves the authenticity of a notary's signature and seal. It is proof of authentication for notarized documents in countries that abide by the 1961 Hague Convention Abolishing the Requirement of Legalization for Foreign Public Documents.

Which of the following is explained above?

A) Apostille
B) Notarial Certificate
C) Certification Authority (CA)
D) Acknowledgment Certificate

24

The oath is a solemn promise, often invoking a divine witness, regarding one's future action or behavior.

For an oath to be effective, in which form must it be?

A) Oral
B) Written
C) Witnessed
D) All of the above

25

To demonstrate genuineness by signing as a witness, which of the following must the notary public do?

A) Authenticate the instrument.
B) Endorse the instrument.
C) Attest the instrument.
D) Certify the instrument.

26

A false certificate is when a person is guilty of issuing official certificates or other official written instruments, and with intent to defraud, deceive or injure another person.

A notary public who knowingly makes a false certificate may be prosecuted for which of the following?

A) Malfeasance
B) Forgery of the official document
C) Misconduct
D) A misdemeanor

27

If an affiant swears falsely, for which of the following he may be prosecuted?

A) Fraud against law
B) Forgery of the official document
C) Committing perjury
D) Counterfeiting

28

Which of the following is a fact of a town official appointed as a notary public?

A) The notary may not retain the fees collected.
B) The expense of his appointment is not a proper town charge.
C) Only non-elected officials may be appointed notaries.
D) Notarial service fees performed for the general public must be split with the town.

29

According to which of the following a notary can certify a copy of a power of attorney?

A) Notary Public Code
B) Probate Code
C) Civil Code
D) Bus. & Prof. Code

30

State of _____

County of _____

The location where the notarial act takes place is usually stated in the above format at the beginning of the notarial certificate.

Which of the following terms is used to refer to the state and county where a notarization takes place?

A) Location
B) Place
C) Site
D) Venue

31

It is a formal written enactment of a legislative authority that governs a state, city or country.

Which of the following is defined above?

A) The Secretary of State
B) Courts of record
C) Statute
D) Tradition

32

Each state sets the fees for notaries public. Under which of the following circumstances is a notary public permitted to receive a higher payment for a service than generally allowed by law?

A) When extra expenses are incurred
B) When the workload is too much
C) When extraordinary circumstances demand it
D) Under no circumstance

33

CLASS OF FELONIES

A : Life imprisonment or death

B : 25 years or more

C : Less than 25 years but 10 or more years

D : Less than 10 years but 5 or more years

E : Less than 5 years but more than 1 year

A notary who executes a false certificate with the intention to defraud or deceive with the knowledge that it contains a false statement/information is guilty of which class of felonies given above?

A) B
B) C
C) D
D) E

34

CLASS OF FELONIES

A : Life imprisonment or death

B : 25 years or more

C : Less than 25 years but 10 or more years

D : Less than 10 years but 5 or more years

E : Less than 5 years but more than 1 year

Forgery is the process of making, adapting, or imitating objects, statistics, or documents with the intent to deceive for the sake of altering the public perception.

A person guilty of forgery in the second degree is guilty of which class of a felony?

A) B
B) C
C) D
D) E

35

Which of the below is a debt instrument, secured by the collateral of specified real estate property, that the borrower is obliged to pay back with a predetermined set of payments?

A) Conveyance
B) Mortgage
C) Escrow
D) Lease

36

Which one below is applicable for taking an acknowledgment and swearing two witnesses?

A) The notary can not charge for it
B) The notary can charge if he travels to the client
C) The notary can charge for it
D) The notary should not charge to elderly

37

A period of how many days does an appointee have to file an oath of office with the county clerk?

A) 7 days
B) 15 days
C) 30 days
D) 90 days

38

An attorney will be prohibited from the office of the notary public in which of the following cases?

A) If he is a resident but not a member of the bar
B) If he is a non-resident and not admitted to practice in the courts of record of this state
C) If he is admitted to practice in the courts of record of this state and moves out of state
D) If he is a non-resident only maintaining an office within this state

39

Which of the following determines the number of notaries public?

A) County clerk
B) The legislature
C) The Secretary of State
D) The city civil service commission (CSC)

40

Which of the following does a notary public have the authority to lawfully do?

A) Execute a will and trust
B) Take the acknowledgment to a legal instrument in which he has a financial report
C) Take the acknowledgment of his constituent
D) Take the acknowledgment of a third party

41

The most critical of the five notary-specific elements on a notarized document is the notary signature. By signing the notary certificate, a notary is verifying that the venue, notary commission expiration date, and the notary certificate are true and correct.

In which color must the signature of the notary public be?

A) Blue
B) Black
C) Blue or black
D) Any color

42

A Notary Public is an official of integrity appointed by state government to serve the public as an impartial witness in performing a variety of official fraud-deterrent acts related to the signing of relevant documents.

Which of the following terms defines a notary public BEST?

A) Amicus curiae
B) Judicial official
C) Legal counselor
D) Ministerial official

43

Deposition testimony is taken orally, with an attorney asking questions and the deponent (the individual being questioned) answering while a court reporter or tape recorder (or sometimes both) records the testimony.

A notary is permitted to take a deposition if he is NOT

A) an attorney for a party or prospective party seeking the examination
B) the employee of an attorney for the party seeking the examination
C) a person with an interest
D) none of the above

44

A will is an official document that says what a person wants to be done with his assets after his death.

Which of the following is the person named in a will to carry out a particular act on the estates?

A) Executor
B) Intestate
C) Administrator
D) Surrogate

45

Which of the following is the act of recognizing the existence of a signed agreement as evidence of one's intention that the agreement is binding and in full force?

A) Acceptance
B) Acknowledgment
C) Notarial act
D) Transaction

46

Within how many days is it mandatory for newly commissioned notaries to file their oath of office and official signature with the county clerk?

A) 7
B) 30
C) 14
D) 21

47

Notaries must complete journal entries at the time of notarization. Which items must always be in the journal?

A) Date, fees, time, type of document
B) Date, type of document, fees
C) Fees, document date, the name of the signer
D) Date, time, fees, thumbprint, the address of the signer

48

Felony is a crime, typically one involving violence regarded as more severe than a misdemeanor, and usually punishable by imprisonment for more than one year or by death.

A felony in another jurisdiction, for the purpose of disqualification from the office of notary public, depends on all of the following except which one?

A) Whether the executive pardon was received
B) The exact nature of the crime
C) The statute upon which the conviction is based
D) If reciprocity exists

Section 1

#	Answer	Topic	Subtopic	#	Answer	Topic	Subtopic	#	Answer	Topic	Subtopic	#	Answer	Topic	Subtopic
1	A	TA	SA2	13	A	TA	SA1	25	C	TB	SB1	37	C	TB	SB1
2	D	TB	SB1	14	D	TA	SA2	26	B	TA	SA1	38	B	TA	SA1
3	C	TA	SA1	15	B	TA	SA1	27	C	TB	SB1	39	C	TA	SA2
4	C	TB	SB1	16	B	TA	SA2	28	B	TA	SA2	40	C	TB	SB1
5	B	TA	SA1	17	D	TB	SB1	29	B	TB	SB1	41	B	TB	SB1
6	A	TB	SB1	18	A	TB	SB2	30	D	TA	SA1	42	D	TB	SB1
7	B	TA	SA1	19	B	TA	SA1	31	C	TA	SA2	43	D	TA	SA1
8	D	TA	SA1	20	D	TB	SB2	32	D	TB	SB2	44	A	TA	SA1
9	D	TB	SB2	21	D	TB	SB1	33	D	TB	SB1	45	B	TB	SB1
10	A	TB	SB2	22	D	TB	SB1	34	C	TA	SA1	46	B	TB	SB1
11	B	TA	SA1	23	A	TA	SA1	35	B	TA	SA1	47	A	TA	SA1
12	B	TB	SB1	24	A	TB	SB1	36	C	TB	SB1	48	D	TA	SA1

Topics & Subtopics

Code	Description	Code	Description
SA1	Basic Concepts	SB2	Duties
SA2	Local Issues	TA	General Knowledge
SB1	Rules	TB	Legal

TEST DIRECTION

DIRECTIONS

Read the questions carefully and then choose the ONE best answer to each question.

Be sure to allocate your time carefully so you are able to complete the entire test within the testing session. You may go back and review your answers at any time.

You may use any available space in your test booklet for scratch work.

Questions in this booklet are not actual test questions but they are the samples for commonly asked questions.

This test aims to cover all topics which may appear on the actual test. However some topics may not be covered.

Studying this booklet will be preparing you for the actual test. It will not guarantee improving your test score but it will help you pass your exam on the first attempt.

Some useful tips for answering multiple choice questions;

- Start with the questions that you can easily answer.

- Underline the keywords in the question.

- Be sure to read all the choices given.

- Watch for keywords such as NOT, always, only, all, never, completely.

- Do not forget to answer every question.

1

The Office of notary public is one of great antiquity and historical significance. It is unclear, however, when or where the first public notary was formally appointed. One of the earliest references to a notary dates back to the time of Cicero.

According to the passage given above, when and where was the office of notary public established?

A) Ancient Greece
B) Medieval England
C) The Roman Empire
D) Colonial America

2

An ex parte decision is one decided by a judge without requiring all of the parties to the controversy to be present.

Which of the following is an ex parte statement?

A) Deposition
B) Acknowledgment
C) Affidavit
D) Conveyance

3

Which of the following is the name given to a person who receives services from a notary public?

A) Client
B) Bearer
C) Advocate
D) Constituent

4

If a notary is unable to communicate with a client, then which of the following should the notary do?

A) Use an interpreter
B) Refer the client to someone who speaks his language
C) Report him to Immigration authorities
D) Notarize any regular documents

5

If it is expected for a notary to sign documents outside their county of residence, he/she may elect to file their oath of office and signature with which of the following?

A) Other county clerks
B) The Secretary of State
C) The State Supreme Court
D) No one needs to know

6

There are many requirements to be a notary public. Because of which of the following a candidate for the office of notary public cannot be appointed?

A) Drunk driving
B) Misdemeanor
C) Possessing burglar's instruments
D) Traffic Offenses

7

Notaries are required to administer oaths in the manner and form prescribed by which of the following?

A) Real Property Law
B) Judiciary Law
C) Public Officers Law
D) Civil Practice Law and Rules

8

When is a county clerk's authentication of notary's authority obtained?

A) When the document specifies a land conveyance
B) When the document is to be used in the County
C) When the document requires such authentication
D) When the document is used outside the State

9

The purpose of an acknowledgment is for a signer, whose identity has been verified, to declare to a Notary or notarial officer that he or she has willingly signed a document.

Which of the following is the thing to be known by the notary in taking an acknowledgment?

A) The facts
B) The reason
C) The truth of the acknowledgment
D) The identity of the maker is the same as the executor

10

An oath is a solemn declaration made according to law, to tell the truth, or to take a specific action.

Which of the following is the equivalent of an oath?

A) Attestation
B) Affirmation
C) Testimony
D) Personal Chattel

11

The primary job duty of a notary is to help prevent fraud by witnessing the signing of documents and verifying their authenticity.

Which of the following is a notary public allowed to do?

A) Making advertisement
B) Drawing up a deed
C) Giving legal advice
D) Executing an acknowledgment of a will

12

What is the maximum length of term for a notary public?

A) Six months
B) One year
C) Two years
D) Four years

13

Sometimes notaries elect to file their signatures so that it makes verification easier.

A certificate of an official character is issued when a notary wants to practice in which of the following?

A) County
B) City
C) States
D) Country

14

Which of the following can a notary public not do on Sunday?

A) Take an acknowledgment
B) Administer an oath
C) Take an affidavit
D) Take a deposition

15

Who does the court administer to the estate of a person that has passed away without leaving a will?

A) Executor
B) Intestate
C) Administrator
D) Surrogate

16

Which of the following defines the agreements made between two parties to do or not to do certain things for legal consideration, whereby each acquires a right to what the other owns?

A) Consideration
B) Bill of sale
C) Contract
D) Lien

17

If a notary public fails to administer an oath, he will be found guilty of which of the following?

A) Remove from office
B) Misdemeanor
C) Felony
D) None of the above

18

In notarial practice, which of the following conditions for a deponent is the most significant?

A) The deponent is who he says he is
B) The deponent is competent
C) The deponent can pay the fee
D) The deponent understands the ramifications of all he is swearing to

CONTINUE ▶

19

Any person not appointed and who conveys that he is a notary public may be prosecuted for which of the following?

A) Misconduct
B) A misdemeanor
C) Perjury
D) A felony

20

A notary public is considered a public officer appointed by a state government. The primary job duty of a notary is to help prevent fraud by witnessing the signing of documents and verifying their authenticity.

Which of the following can a notary not do?

A) Administer Oaths
B) Perform Marriages
C) Charge for his services
D) Take an acknowledgment on a conveyance

21

If an individual wishes to sue a non-resident notary public, the summons may be served upon which of the following?

A) County clerk
B) Attorney general
C) Secretary of State
D) Notary only

22

Which of the below is not the duty of the notary public?

A) Swearing to an affirmation
B) Signing off on an acknowledgment
C) Signing off on a deposition
D) Formation of a will

23

Which of the following is a requirement to be appointed as a notary public?

A) United States citizenship
B) Residence of the state
C) Having a place of business in the state
D) Registering as a voter

24

Attestation is the act of showing or evidence showing that something is accurate and factual. It refers to a third party recognition of a documented agreement's validity.

Which of the following performs the attestation?

A) Attorney
B) Witness
C) Deponent
D) Litigant

25

Notary public fees are determined by which of the following?

A) The law
B) Each notary sets his fee
C) The fee is determined by agreement
D) Each notary sets his fee except in cases in which he is employed

26

An indictment is a formal accusation that a person has committed a crime.

If a notary charges for services more than the law allows him, he is subject to indictment. Which of the following would he not be indicted with?

A) Criminal contempt
B) Treble damages
C) Criminal prosecution
D) Felony

27

If the notary is notarizing a document for a personal friend, which of the following must be included in the journal?

A) Driver license number of the signer
B) Fee for the notary
C) Type of the document notarized
D) All of the above

28

Which of the following is the name given to the section of the state law which requires certain contracts MUST be in writing or partially complied with to be enforceable at law?

A) Proof clause
B) Contract law
C) Common law
D) Statute of frauds

29

When a Notary changes a business address to a new county within the state, which of the following must the notary do?

A) Inform the Secretary of State of the address change
B) File a new oath of office and amendment to the Notary's bond.
C) Change the name of the county in the Notary's seal.
D) All of the above

30

In the law of the United States, a deposition is the (out-of-court) oral testimony of a witness. Which of the following is a name given to a deposition?

A) Affair
B) Attestator
C) Deponent
D) Depositor

31

If the lessee of a safe deposit box doesn't pay the rental fee or doesn't empty the box after the prescribed period by the law, the box may be opened by a notary accompanied by which of the following?

A) Locksmith
B) County clerk
C) Bank guard
D) Bank officer

32

A duly qualified notary public is considered capable of performing notarial duties by which of the following?

A) Rules of the Secretary of State
B) Rules of the Governor
C) Dictates of his conscience
D) The law

33

The jurisdiction of a notary public broadens throughout which of the following?

A) United States
B) State only
C) County of residence
D) City of residence

34

Conveyance is the act of transferring an ownership interest in real property from one party to another. Conveyance also refers to the written instrument, such as a deed or lease that transfers legal title of a property from the seller to the buyer.

Before which of the following the acknowledgment or proof of a conveyance of real property may not be made?

A) Real estate broker
B) Justice of the Supreme Court
C) Title examiner
D) Notary public

35

Which of the following is not correct?

A) The deed is a document by which a person conveys (transfers) real property.
B) Affiant is the person making an affidavit.
C) A felony is a lesser crime than a misdemeanor.
D) The transfer, surrender, or assignment of any interest in real property is called a conveyance.

36

For which of the following a Notary may not charge a fee for notarization?

A) Quitclaim deed
B) Circulator's affidavit
C) Power of attorney
D) Affidavit of support

37

Which of the following is the process of giving sworn evidence and document used as testimony in court proceedings?

A) Write
B) Instrument
C) Deposition
D) Subpoena

38

If a notary public practices any fraudulent activity or deceitful acts in his performance duties he can be convicted of which of the following?

A) Misconduct
B) A misdemeanor
C) Malpractice
D) A felony

39

A subscribing witness is one who sees writing executed or hears it acknowledged, and at the request of the party thereupon signs his name as a witness.

Who is the subscribing witness to any instrument verified or acknowledged before a notary public?

A) Notary public
B) Constituent
C) Affiant
D) Maker

40

An individual might become a notary public if his appointment was revoked by failure to file within the specified period by which of the following?

A) Reapplying
B) Paying a fee
C) Reapplying and paying a fee
D) Reapplying and passing the qualifying exam

41

Which of the following is correct for a county clerk's certificate of official character?

A) No fee is required
B) Notary need to pay a fee
C) Notary pays if he makes over $50K per year
D) The notary does not pay if he is over the age of 65

42

The contents in a safe deposit box after the expiration of ten years from the time of opening of the box will be deemed _____ property

A) lost
B) government
C) destroyed
D) abandoned

43

A county clerk is an elected county official who is responsible for local elections and maintaining public records.

The signature and seal of a county clerk upon a certificate of the official character of a notary public may be in which of the following format?

A) Printed
B) Photographed
C) Engraved
D) All of the above

44

It is a "lesser" criminal act in some common law legal systems. It is considered a crime of low seriousness. Mostly it is punished with monetary fines.

A person who depicts himself as a notary will be guilty of the crime described above.

Which of the following is the name given to this crime?

A) Misdemeanor
B) Felony
C) Harassment
D) Perjury

45

The impediment is a hindrance or obstruction in doing something.

Which of the following is a legal impediment to a person being appointed to the office of a notary public?

A) Illegally using or carrying a pistol
B) Receiving or having criminal possession of stolen property
C) Unlawful possession of a habit-forming narcotic drug
D) All of the above

46

If a person does not file his oath of office within the prescribed time, his appointment is revoked.

Which of the following given below does he have to do now?

A) Paying the fee
B) Reapplying and paying the fee
C) Reapplying only
D) Passing the examination

47

A stockholder is an individual, group, or organization that holds one or more shares in a company, and in whose name the share certificate is issued. It's also known as the shareholder.

Which of the following may a notary who is a stockholder of a corporation do?

A) Not protesting for the non-acceptance of negotiable instruments owned by the corporation
B) Not protesting for the non-payment of negotiable instruments owned by the corporation
C) Protesting for the non-acceptance and non-payment of negotiable instruments owned or held for collection by that corporation
D) Protesting for the non-acceptance and non-payment of negotiable instruments held for collection by the corporation

48

Within how many months after military discharge a notary public who has neglected to reapply for appointment on account of enlistment in the armed forces should apply for reappointment?

A) One month
B) Three months
C) Six months
D) Twelve months

Section 2

#	Answer	Topic	Subtopic	#	Answer	Topic	Subtopic	#	Answer	Topic	Subtopic	#	Answer	Topic	Subtopic
1	C	TA	SA1	13	A	TA	SA2	25	D	TB	SB1	37	C	TB	SB1
2	C	TA	SA1	14	D	TB	SB1	26	A	TB	SB1	38	B	TB	SB1
3	D	TA	SA1	15	C	TA	SA1	27	D	TB	SB2	39	A	TA	SA1
4	B	TA	SA1	16	C	TA	SA1	28	D	TB	SB1	40	C	TB	SB1
5	A	TA	SA2	17	B	TA	SA1	29	A	TA	SA1	41	D	TB	SB1
6	C	TA	SA1	18	A	TB	SB1	30	C	TB	SB1	42	D	TA	SA1
7	D	TB	SB1	19	B	TA	SA1	31	D	TB	SB2	43	D	TB	SB2
8	D	TB	SB1	20	B	TB	SB1	32	D	TB	SB1	44	A	TA	SA1
9	B	TA	SA1	21	C	TA	SA2	33	B	TA	SA2	45	D	TB	SB1
10	B	TB	SB1	22	D	TB	SB2	34	A	TA	SA1	46	B	TB	SB2
11	A	TB	SB1	23	A	TB	SB1	35	C	TA	SA1	47	C	TA	SA1
12	D	TB	SB1	24	B	TB	SB1	36	B	TB	SB1	48	D	TB	SB2

Topics & Subtopics

Code	Description
SA1	Basic Concepts
SA2	Local Issues
SB1	Rules

Code	Description
SB2	Duties
TA	General Knowledge
TB	Legal

CONTINUE ▶

TEST DIRECTION

DIRECTIONS

Read the questions carefully and then choose the ONE best answer to each question.

Be sure to allocate your time carefully so you are able to complete the entire test within the testing session. You may go back and review your answers at any time.

You may use any available space in your test booklet for scratch work.

Questions in this booklet are not actual test questions but they are the samples for commonly asked questions.

This test aims to cover all topics which may appear on the actual test. However some topics may not be covered.

Studying this booklet will be preparing you for the actual test. It will not guarantee improving your test score but it will help you pass your exam on the first attempt.

Some useful tips for answering multiple choice questions;

- Start with the questions that you can easily answer.

- Underline the keywords in the question.

- Be sure to read all the choices given.

- Watch for keywords such as NOT, always, only, all, never, completely.

- Do not forget to answer every question.

1.

A notary who practice law may, besides being removed from office be punished for which of the following?

A) Slander
B) Libel
C) Felony
D) Criminal contempt

2.

Which of the following notaries do not need to record in their journals?

A) The date and time of notarization
B) The fees charged for a notarial services
C) Type of the document notarized
D) The signer's address

3.

A non-attorney notary (qualified & bonded as an immigration consultant) may charge up to $10 for which of the following?

A) Per signature on a Jurat
B) Oaths and affirmation
C) Completing immigration application
D) All of the above

4.

What is the educational requirement to become a notary public?

A) Common school education
B) High school diploma
C) College degree
D) Masters degree

5

In the law of evidence, a credible witness is a person making testimony in a court or other tribunal or acting otherwise as a witness, whose credibility is unimpeachable. Several factors affect witnesses' credibility. A credible witness is "competent to give evidence, and is worthy of belief."

Which of the following is correct about Credible witnesses?

A) They are never placed under oath
B) They must not have a financial interest in the document
C) They must always know the notary
D) All of the above

6

Satisfactory evidence would include credible witnesses. A credible witness is a person who knows the signer who is willing to swear under oath as to the identity of the signer.

Satisfactory evidence of identity means relying on either which of the following?

A) ID cards
B) Credible identifying witnesses
C) Business card photos
D) Both ID cards and Credible identifying witnesses

7

A certificate must be included with each notarial act. The certificate must:

- Be executed at the same time as the performance of the notarial act;

- Be signed and dated by the notary;

- Be signed in the same manner as on file with the Secretary of State;

- Identify the jurisdiction (state and county) in which the notarial act was performed; and

- Contain a clear impression of the notary's official stamping device, which includes the commission expiration date.

If you request a new Certificate of Authorization, the State must respond within how many days?

A) 5 days
B) 10 days
C) 14 days
D) 30 days

8

Which of the following is signed in the presence of the notary?

A) Certificate
B) Jurat
C) Acknowledgment
D) All of the above

CONTINUE ▶

9

The evidence of a personal debt secured by real property is usually in the form of which of the following?

A) Mortgage
B) Lien
C) Lease
D) Bond

10

Journal of notarial acts refers to the notary public's sequential record of notarial transactions. It is a bound book listing the date, time, and type of each official act. It records the signature of each person whose signature is notarized.

Journal of notarial acts also records the type of information used to verify the identity of parties whose signatures are notarized, and the fee charged. It is also used as evidence in court. Journal of notarial acts is also known as a notarial record, notarial register, or notary record book.

Which of the following is not true about the journal of the notarial act?

A) Some states require a journal's format to include certain features.
B) It contains details of the transaction in the event a notarized document is lost, altered, or if facts concerning the notarization are challenged in court.
C) Most states do not require that Notaries own and maintain a journal or record book of the acts they perform.
D) It is an important tool that provides a written record of the Notary's official acts.

11

"Falsifying documents" is a type of white-collar crime. It involves altering, changing, or modifying a document to deceive another person. It can also involve the passing along of copies of documents that are known to be false. In many states, falsifying a document is a crime punishable as a felony.

If a notary willingly and knowingly notarizes a real estate document that he knows to be fraudulent, he will be guilty of which of the following?

A) Misdemeanor
B) Lis pendens
C) Carpe diem
D) Felony

12

Which of the following is a requirement for becoming a State Notary Public?

A) Being under 18 years of age
B) Having a criminal record
C) Working in the state at least 1 year
D) Being a legal resident of the state

13

Every one commits perjury who, with intent to mislead, makes before a person who is authorized by law to permit it to be made before him a false statement under oath or solemn affirmation, by affidavit, solemn declaration or deposition or orally, knowing that the statement is false.

Which of the following is a possible penalty for committing perjury?

A) Two years in prison
B) Three years in prison
C) Four years in prison
D) Any of the above

14

If a notary public resigns a position with the employer what must he do?

A) He must resign his commission
B) Leave all journals with the employer for the new notary
C) Retake the exam
D) Notify the Secretary of State of any business address change

15

Which of the following is a possible size of the stamp?

A) A 6-foot diameter
B) 1 inch in width by 2 ½ inches in length
C) 2 ½ inches by 6 inches
D) One foot square

16

A notary is obligated to do which of the following?

A) Reimburse a surety company for bond funds paid out
B) Determine whether a signer has authority to sign as a corporate officer
C) Let their employer hold their seal if they paid for it.
D) Use the all-purpose certificate for a jurat.

17

Which of the following is the fee for notarizing a circulator's affidavit?

A) $0
B) $5.00
C) $20.00
D) Negotiable

18

When a notary is employed by a city, county or state agency, what happens to the fees collected for non-agency related notarization?

A) It will be kept by the Notary
B) It will be turned over to a supervisor
C) Remitted by the Notary Public to the employing agency
D) It will always be free

19

Which of the following may a notary do?

A) Advertise he is an immigration consultant
B) Take depositions and affidavits
C) Normally notarize a will
D) Certify a copy of a foreign birth certificate

20

Incumbent means "necessary for someone as a duty or responsibility"

Incumbent comes from the Latin word *incumbens*, which means lying in or leaning on, but came to mean holding a position. It was first used in English for someone holding a church office, and then someone holding any office.

For which of the following it is incumbent on the notary to scrutinize each document presented?

A) To ensure it is in the form prescribed by law
B) To determine if an oath is required
C) To see that the person who executed the instrument has not signed his name without the presence of the notary
D) To determine the exact nature of his duty concerning the document

21

When will a notary public not be disqualified automatically from doing a notarization?

A) When he becomes a Lessor
B) When he becomes a Vendee
C) When he becomes a Real Estate Agent
D) When he becomes a Grantor

22

Notarial act means Action performed by a notary public in his or her official capacity, such as in authenticating a document by witnessing it and placing the notarial seal on it.

Which of the following acts are all Notary Actions?

A) Copy Certification, Acknowledgment, Oath, Deposition
B) Loan Document Signing, Jurat, Affirmation, Protest, Power of Attorney
C) Affidavit, Proof of Execution, Protest, Jurat
D) Acknowledgment, Proof of Execution, Jurat, Oath of Office

23

When is it not illegal to take an acknowledgment over the telephone?

A) It is always illegal.
B) When the notary has satisfactory evidence that the person making it is the person described
C) When jurat is not required
D) When the venue is not an issue

24

Jurisdiction is the official power to make legal decisions and judgments. After you become a Notary Public, which of the following will be your jurisdiction?

A) The entire state of the State
B) The city in which you work
C) The county in which you live
D) The entire United States

25

Which of the following agency of the State gives the new certificate of Notary Public?

A) Corporation Commissioner
B) Bureau of Notary Publics
C) Secretary of State
D) Department of Real Estate

26

How many people write the name of the X signer during the signature by mark process?

A) One
B) Two
C) At least two
D) None of the above

27

The Notary seal is the impression of the Notary Public inked stamp or crimping embossed and is used to authenticate the Notary's signature and make the notarial act official. The term Notary seal can also refer to your stamp or embosser.

Where do the notaries obtain their seals from?

A) Secretary of State
B) County Clerk
C) Approved vendors or manufacturers
D) Their employer

28

When does someone officially become a notary public?

A) After passing the exam
B) When the Secretary of State sends the commission
C) After getting the first certificate
D) After oath and bond are filed

29

Which of the following is the county named in the Venue?

A) The place where the signer personally appeared
B) The place where the notary's business is located
C) The place where the signer lives
D) None of the above

30

A notary may do which of the following?

A) Notarize a document in a foreign language
B) Not notarize documents that he or she will sign as corporate officers
C) Notarize friend's documents
D) All of the above

31

If a Notary moves, within how many days must he contact the proper authority?

A) One day
B) Ten days
C) 30 days
D) 180 days

32

Notario Público

The problem arises when individuals obtain a notary public license in the United States and use that license to substantiate representations that they are a "notario publico" to immigrant populations that ascribe a vastly different meaning to the term.

Which of the following about using the words "notario publico" is correct?

A) It is encouraged
B) It is legal in some states
C) It is prohibited
D) It indicates a lingual ability

33

Escrow is a legal concept in which a third party holds a financial instrument or an asset on behalf of two other parties that are in the process of completing a transaction.

Escrows should be revocable by which of the following?

A) The first party
B) The escrowee
C) Either party
D) No one needs to know

34

When a notary can not notarize a document?

A) If he is an agent for the document
B) If he is an employer
C) If he is the lawyer for the document
D) If he is trustor or trustee of the document

35

A notary public must file an oath of office and bond with the county clerk's office in the county where their principal place of business is located. It is recommended that the oath and bond be submitted in person to guarantee timely filing.

After your commencement date, how many days do you have to take your oath of office?

A) Six months
B) Ten days
C) Thirty days
D) None of the above

36

A notary who is a member of the state bar may take the affidavit of his client concerning any matters when it is taken

A) before a pending cause
B) with the permission of the court of record
C) before the suit commences
D) in his discretion

37

Which of the following is a correct statement?

A) The notary has to draft power of attorney, mortgages, and deeds when requested
B) A notary does not have to charge a fee
C) Holographic wills must be notarized to be valid
D) Holographic wills are typewritten

38

Where can a notary get a certificate of authorization from?

A) The governor's office
B) The Department of Real Estate
C) The Secretary of State
D) None of the above

39

A subscribing witness could also be used in a "Proof of Execution" to swear that they witnessed another particular person signed a document."

Which of the following can s subscribing witness can bring you?

A) Quit Claim Deed
B) Grant Deed
C) Mortgage
D) Homestead Declaration

40

Notary seal is the impression of the Notary Public inked stamp or crimping embossed and is used to authenticate the Notary's signature and make the notarial act official. The term Notary seal can also refer to your stamp or embosser.

Which of the following is the shape of notary stamp?

A) Triangle
B) Rectangular
C) Only a circle
D) None of the above

41

In the law of evidence, a credible witness is a person making testimony in a court or other tribunal or acting otherwise as a witness, whose credibility is unimpeachable.

Which of the following is true about two credible witnesses?

A) Two credible witnesses are not allowed
B) They must be over 21
C) They must be fingerprinted
D) None of the above

42

Which of the following is the fine for failing to post signs that you are not an attorney and cannot give legal advice?

A) Three – five years in the prison
B) Up to $1,500 fine and at least one-year suspension of commission for the first time and for the second time permanent revocation of commission
C) Up to $7,500 fine
D) $100,000 fine

43

A certified copy is a copy (often a photocopy) of a primary document, that has on it an endorsement or certificate that it is an exact copy of the primary document. It does not certify that the primary document is genuine, only that it is a real copy of the primary document.

Which of the following does a certified copy certify for the reproduction?

A) It states that the reproduction is a real copy of the primary document.
B) It states that the primary document is genuine.
C) It is the same as the original document.
D) None of the above

44

Journal of notarial acts refers to notary public's sequential record of notarial transactions. Generally, it is a bound book listing the date, time, and type of each official act. It records the signature of each person whose signature is notarized.

If you give up your journal to a proper authority, you must notify the Secretary of State within how many days?

A) One day
B) Seven days
C) Ten days
D) Fourteen days

45

The Official Notary seal stamp or seal embosser is the most-used tool of a Notary. The Notary seal is the impression of the Notary Public inked stamp or crimping embossed. It is used to authenticate the Notary's signature and make the notarial act official.

Which of the following is true about an embossed seal impression?

A) It is always required by Notary Law
B) It can never be used
C) It is acceptable but not required
D) It is only for senior notaries

CONTINUE ▶

46

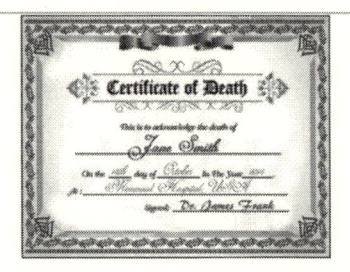

A death certificate is an official statement, signed by a physician, of the cause, date, and place of a person's death.

Which of the following about death certificate is correct?

A) It must be notarized
B) It is not notarized
C) The IRS files it
D) All of the above

47

The unauthorized practice of law is engaging in the practice of law by persons or entities not authorized to practice law according to state law.

Using the designations "lawyer", "attorney at law", counselor at law," "law", "law office", "J.D." ,"Esq." or other equivalent words by any person or entity who is not authorized is also an unauthorized practice of law.

A Notary who engages in the unauthorized practice of law may face which of the following?

A) Commission denial
B) Commission revocation
C) Commission suspension
D) All of the above

Most U.S. states and jurisdictions only authorize commissioned Notaries Public or other notarial officers recognized under state law to perform notarial acts within the borders of the commissioning state or jurisdiction.

A notary commissioned by the state may perform notarizations anywhere within the state's borders, but may not perform a notarization in another state.

If a notary public moves to another state, where must he apply to be authorized?

A) Secretary of State
B) Notary commission
C) County Clerk
D) Department of Notary Public

Section 3

#	Answer	Topic	Subtopic	#	Answer	Topic	Subtopic	#	Answer	Topic	Subtopic	#	Answer	Topic	Subtopic
1	D	TA	SA1	13	D	TB	SB1	25	C	TA	SA2	37	D	TB	SB2
2	D	TB	SB1	14	D	TB	SB2	26	C	TB	SB1	38	C	TB	SB2
3	D	TA	SA1	15	B	TA	SA1	27	C	TA	SA2	39	D	TA	SA1
4	A	TB	SB1	16	A	TB	SB2	28	D	TB	SB2	40	B	TA	SA1
5	B	TA	SA2	17	A	TB	SB1	29	A	TA	SA2	41	D	TA	SA1
6	D	TB	SB2	18	C	TB	SB2	30	D	TB	SB2	42	B	TB	SB1
7	B	TA	SA2	19	B	TA	SA2	31	C	TA	SA2	43	A	TA	SA1
8	B	TA	SA1	20	D	TB	SB1	32	C	TA	SA2	44	B	TA	SA1
9	D	TA	SA1	21	C	TB	SB2	33	D	TB	SB1	45	C	TA	SA2
10	C	TB	SB2	22	D	TA	SA2	34	D	TB	SB1	46	B	TA	SA1
11	D	TB	SB1	23	A	TB	SB2	35	C	TB	SB2	47	D	TB	SB2
12	D	TB	SB1	24	A	TA	SA2	36	D	TA	SA1	48	A	TA	SA2

Topics & Subtopics

Code	Description	Code	Description
SA1	Basic Concepts	SB2	Duties
SA2	Local Issues	TA	General Knowledge
SB1	Rules	TB	Legal

Made in the USA
Monee, IL
01 February 2022